HOW TO WEAR

With Style

HOW TO WEAR HATS
With Style

DONA MUNKER

Illustrations by Suzanne Barraza

With Photographs by Roger Prigent

Prince Paperbacks / Crown Publishers, Inc. New York

Hats by the following: Betmar Hats—pages 31 (top), 34 (top and middle), 35 (bottom),37 (bottom), 40 (top), 58, 59 (top),62, 63; Patricia Underwood—pages 30, 46 (top), 50, 51, 55 (top); Albrizio Hats—pages 34 (bottom), 40 (bottom), 47 (bottom), 54, 55 (bottom); Archie Eason—pages 35 (top), 37 (top), 43 (bottom), 46 (bottom), 47 (top), 59 (bottom).

In some cases it has proved impossible to identify the models appearing in several of the photographs in this book, despite every effort to do so. The publisher would like to hear from the models concerned in order to ensure credit in future editions.

All photographs by Roger Prigent, courtesy of Roger Prigent and Frank Olive's World, and also courtesy of the following: page 28 courtesy of H. V. Models; pages 36 and 44 courtesy of Dawn Ann and Ford Models; page 38 courtesy of Sharlene Walter; page 48 courtesy of Laura Roberson and Ford Models; page 56 courtesy of Lisa Hinkle and the Nancy Bounds Agency.

Pages 6—12 courtesy of the Millinery Institute of America; pages 19—20 courtesy of Betmar Hats.

Published by Crown Publishers, Inc., 225 Park Avenue South, New York, New York 10003 and represented in Canada by the Canadian MANDA group.
CROWN, PRINCE PAPERBACKS, and colophon are trademarks of Crown Publishers, Inc.

Manufactured in the United States of America

Design by Lauren Dong

Library of Congress Cataloging-in-Publication Data

Munker, Dona.
   How to wear hats with style.

   (Prince paperbacks)
   1. Hats. I. Title.
TT665.M83   1988   646   87-15531
ISBN 0-517-56760-1

10 9 8 7 6 5 4 3 2 1

First Edition

Contents

Acknowledgments

Warm thanks for much kind help and advice to Bernard Grossman and Bernadette Rosenstadt of Betmar Hats, and to Marsha Akins, Ann Albrizio, Ellen Brody, Archie Eason, Georgine Harabin, David Stein, and Patricia Underwood. Thanks also to Burt Champion of the Millinery Institute of America; Lois Fine of Adolpho; Rusty Donovan of Ford Models; Suzanne Newman of Josephine Tripoli, New York; and to Lisa Healy and Kate Schwinghammer of Crown Publishers.

Very special thanks to photographer Roger Prigent and to a tireless, generous spokesman for a craft he loves, Frank Olive.

Introduction: Cultivating the Right Hattitude

A hat isn't just another accessory. It's a mood, an image, a state of mind. It's a message from you to the world. It can pull a whole outfit together. It can express your true personality, or let you don as many different moods and personalities as you have hats.

Can *you* wear a hat? The answer is certainly yes—even if you've never worn one before. All the experts agree that any woman can wear a hat, if it's the right one for her individual features. And "any woman" means just that: a woman with a long face or a round one; a petite woman or one who's built like a Rubens goddess; a woman who wears glasses or a woman with a long nose.

This book tells you all you need to know about looking for a hat, trying it on, and wearing it. It tells you about quality and care. It gives you the advice of renowned designers like Marsha Akins, Ann Albrizio, Archie Eason, Frank Olive, and Patricia Underwood, and it even answers your questions about hat etiquette. Most important, it teaches you how to become an expert at spotting the hats that are perfect for *you*.

There's nothing mysterious about wearing hats—after all, women have been doing it for hundreds of years! You can easily develop an eye for the hats that are right for your individual style and face. The trick (as with your other clothes) is to know a few simple guidelines to cultivate your own "hat sense."

That's where the special illustrations in the second half of this book come in. By actually looking at examples of a wide range of hats from famous milliners such as Archie Eason, Albrizio, Betmar Hats, Frank Olive's World, and Patricia Underwood, you'll be able to start getting ideas about what you like and what will look right on you.

Armed with the hundreds of tips and suggestions in this book, you can wear hats with confidence and flair, create your own highly personal and individual style, and develop a look that makes you feel chic and special.

Once you've learned to look like the woman you want to be—and to enjoy all the compliments she'll get—you may never want to go out without a hat again!

Part 1

WHAT ARE YOU LOOKING FOR?

There are lots of reasons for buying a hat—practical and personal reasons. Maybe you want something to give a touch of extra class to that coat you wear all the time. Or something that will pull a favorite outfit together, rounding it off and "balancing" it as well. Or perhaps you want a way to keep your head warm—or dry, or cool— that will give you a lift at the same time.

The key to glorious hat-wearing is to start out *knowing what you're looking for*. Especially if you're a beginning hat buyer (or a not-so-beginning one with six hats in the closet that you've never worn), here are a few questions to think about *before* you get into serious searching.

WHAT ARE YOU GOING TO WEAR IT WITH?

Have a clear idea of what clothes the hat is meant to go with. A hat that doesn't complement at least one outfit in your wardrobe is a hat that will molder on the closet shelf for all eternity.

THE GENERAL-PURPOSE HAT

If you're buying your first or second hat, you're probably looking for something to wear with several outfits—say, a coat, a suit, and one or two dresses (of which maybe one does double duty for daytime wear and after-hours socializing). If so, you should be looking for a versatile hat that enhances these clothes, one that is pretty, but not so unusual that you will get tired of wearing it.

• Take a good look at your wardrobe. You'll probably find that it has what designers call a "color premise"—the colors you naturally gravitate to. "A good wardrobe," says Marsha Akins, who designs the well-known line of Makins Hats, "has one or two basic colors. Good accessories, hats included, work in a circle; they're flexible enough to complement most of the clothes you normally wear." *Think about the colors hanging in your closet and choose a basic hat that works well with the colors you wear most often.*

• Think, too, about your essential "fashion self." *What kind of image and lifestyle do your clothes reflect?* Are you basically the tailored type? Frilly and romantic? Trendy? Casual-to-funky? If you're buying a hat to round off outfits that project a certain image (and most outfits do that), you'll need a hat that suits the image with which you feel happiest, given your age, lifestyle, and personality.

• *For what kinds of occasions do you plan to wear the hat?* Will it be mainly a hat you throw on to wear to a movie with pals? Something to wear to business lunches? To church or synagogue? Think about the range of occasions you'll probably wear it for *before* you start looking.

THE ONE-OCCASION OR ONE-OUTFIT HAT

Not all of us can afford such a luxury, and if you love a hat (and you shouldn't buy one you *don't* love), you'll want to wear it more than once, and probably with more than just one outfit—which a good hat will outlast anyway. So if you're on your way to the store to hunt down a very special hat for that stunning new silk dress or that once-in-a-lifetime party, here are some thoughts:

• Ask yourself whether you'll be able to wear the hat with anything else. The answer to this question doesn't have to be yes—if you find a hat that looks fabulous on you and you can afford it, perhaps you should buy it even if you can only wear it with one dress. On the other hand, if your pocketbook doesn't permit that, look for a hat that will enhance one or two other outfits as well.

• If you want the hat for a single, special occasion, and you aren't rich, make up your mind that the hat you buy will be one for which other uses can be found later.

• Especially if you have only one-time immediate plans for the hat, keep in mind that it should be appropriate to the occasion (a Portrait hat with a six-inch drooping brim might not be the best choice for a movie, right?) and should feel natural on you. You want to have a good time and feel comfortable, not somehow silly or conspicuous. A single-occasion hat, like any other, should be one that suits the real you.

• And, of course, keep in mind that it's vital to know whether the hat you select will do what it's meant to do for the outfit it's supposed to enhance. So, if possible, wear the outfit when you're shopping for the hat.

WHAT PSYCHOLOGICAL PURPOSE IS THE HAT TO SERVE?

You *can* buy a hat solely for warmth, shade, or rain gear, but what a waste! A good hat does more than protect your head or even round off a suit of clothes—its other aim is to make you feel that you're the woman you want to be.

Before you buy, therefore, figure out what the *mental* benefits are supposed to be. Maybe you're buying this hat to make heads turn at a dance—or perhaps you want it to hide you from prying glances. Perhaps you want it to transform you from a hard-working businesswoman into a fatal charmer fluttering her eyelashes at a new date. Maybe you secretly want it to change you from a fresh-faced kid into the "bohemian artist" you are at heart. Maybe you just want to feel—well, *different*.

Whatever you want it for, keep in mind that, once it's on your head, your hat projects a certain image and becomes an extension of your own personality. You'll choose hats with confidence if you know what you want that personality to be—and are realistic about how comfortable you'll feel with the choice. *Look for a hat that can enhance the woman you are,* not one that you aren't.

On the other hand, this doesn't mean that you shouldn't experiment! On the contrary—how are you going to find out what hats are right for you unless you give yourself a chance to explore all the possibilities when you shop?

PRE-SHOPPING

So don't limit yourself in advance by assuming that you "can't wear" certain types of hats. Window shop. Consider what you see—whether you like it, how it would look on you, how it would work with the outfits you have in mind. Look everywhere and at everything you come across. Frank Olive, whose creations have appeared on such notables as Claudette Colbert and Lee Remick, advises his clients to look at hats not only on store window mannequins but also on models in television commercials and magazine ads to start developing an eye for what they think they'd like.

Looking around, cautions Patricia Underwood, another noted New York designer, means *looking at the hat itself*—not at dazzling decorations. "Think about the basic shape," says Ms. Underwood, "not the trim. You're looking for the complete design, not a pretty flower that's been tacked on."

The same advice, of course, applies when you actually go out to buy a hat. But before you do, one more simple suggestion:

BUY A HAT THAT FITS!

There are probably millions of American women with hats sitting in the boxes they were brought home in because they turned out to be "a little snug," after all.

Never, never buy a hat that is too small for your head. "I don't care how pretty it looks," says Patricia Underwood; "if it doesn't fit, you've wasted your money." Although some felt hats can be stretched slightly by a professional milliner, it's all but impossible to enlarge most hats. And a too-tight hat is an unworn hat. It will end up in the closet along with the miniature beer steins Aunt Betsy brought you from Disney World.

Prospects are better for a hat that is too large, since it's possible for a professional hat maker to make a large hat smaller by adjusting the band.

To determine your hat size, start at the center of your upper forehead and measure the circumference of your head, about an inch above the ears and back around the crown at its widest point (where the brim of the hat will rest). Don't push your hair aside, since the hat has to cover that, too. Women's hat sizes, which are described in inches, range from about 22″ to 24″, with the average range about 22½″ to 23½″.

Unless your hat is being custom-made, however, you don't really need to know your size—the test will come in the store. A hat that fits will slip easily down onto your head. Its crown will generally ride close to the top of your head (unless the crown is extra high), and the brim will rest comfortably on your forehead, not pinch it. (More about all this in "Trying It On in the Store.")

BASIC SHAPES AND STYLES

There are hundreds of variations on crowns and brims, and since quality hats each have an individual design hardly any generalizations can be made about what "style" will look good on an individual woman. But knowing something about a few basic shapes is a great confidence builder! So here's a rundown on some popular styles:

THE SHEPHERDESS

This hat got its name about three hundred years ago when it was worn—you guessed it—by girls who looked after sheep and needed sunshades. The brim slopes down to shade the brow, and the crown may be either rounded or shallow.

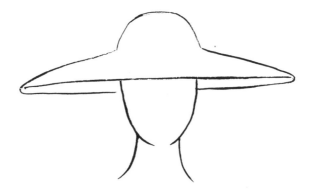

THE PORTRAIT (OR PICTURE) HAT

This is the great haute couture hat, beloved of European designers from Balenciaga to Lagerfeld. The name, of course, comes from the extra-wide brim that frames the face as though in a picture.

Portraits may be casual and informal, or elegant, even extravagant. Their impact is always dramatic. They are best worn by medium-to-tall women, but shorter women may be able to wear similar styles with proportioned brims (see "Picture This Face").

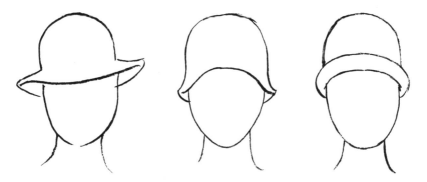

THE CLOCHE

One of the most common styles, the Cloche's basic feature is its deep, rounded crown, which fits closely against the head and is worn well down on the forehead. It may have a *small brim* (shown) or a medium one, or it may be *brimless* (shown). It may also have a *rolled brim* (shown).

THE FEDORA

A men's hat style that is now worn by women. Its features are a high, indented crown with a medium-to-wide brim.

A Western (or Cowboy) is a Fedora with a wider brim that is turned up at the sides.

THE DERBY

A variation of an English men's style (the Bowler, with its deep, rounded crown), the Derby's distinctive feature is a brim that is rolled up on the sides. The term has come to be used for any small, sporty hat with the side brim rolled.

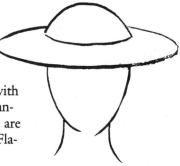

THE PADRE

Originally a sunshade for Spanish priests, the Padre features a crown with a large, flat brim. Other popular Spanish men's hat styles worn by women are the shallow-crowned, flat-brimmed Flamenco and Gaucho styles.

THE SCOTTIE

Another male hat taken over by the ladies, the perky Scottie is actually based on a Highlander's military cap.

THE SAILOR (OR BOATER)

Another Anglo-Saxon gent's style (originally a sailor's hat that later came to be worn for boating on the river) that's now a feminine favorite. Straw Sailors (Boaters) are popular as casual spring and summer hats. This simple style, with its flat, shallow crown and small-to-medium brim, looks good with many different shapes of faces.

THE CAP

A Cap is any small, brimless, close-fitting hat that covers the crown of the head. There are countless varieties. Among them: the tiny Juliette Cap that perches well back on the wearer's crown and may serve as no more than an excuse for a cloud of pretty netting; the diamond-shaped Teardrop (or "Alexis") Cap (see photograph on page 48); the Visored Cap (shown); the larger Cheek-to-Cheek knitted types that reach the ears and can be pulled down over them for warmth.

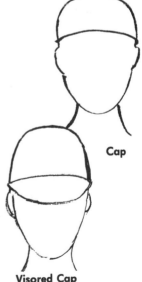

Cap

Visored Cap

THE PILLBOX

A hardy perennial, the Pillbox is a small round or squared brimless hat that sits on top of the head. Jacqueline Kennedy made this the favorite style of the 1960s. Still popular, it is presently worn forward and angled sideways, rather than at the back of the crown.

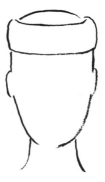

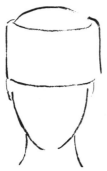

THE TOQUE

Essentially a tall Pillbox, often with an indented crown. A variation is the even higher Russian Toque (or Shako), familiar as the "Dr. Zhivago" hat.

THE FEZ

Originally Turkish, this men's hat has been popular with women for hundreds of years.

THE TURBAN

Another hat with a whiff of the Near East to it. A true Turban "closes" above the center of the forehead—otherwise it's really a Helmet, or a Wrapped Hat, posing as a Turban. Despite its exotic air, this is a surprisingly versatile style.

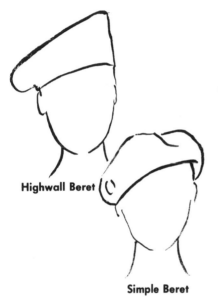

Highwall Beret

Simple Beret

THE BERET

One of the most popular styles, the Beret—according to designer and noted millinery authority Ann Albrizio—was probably history's first hat. It has many varieties. Shown here are two, a simple Beret and a Highwall Beret.

THE HEADWRAP

Cross a hat with a scarf and a headband and you get a Headwrap. Not really a hat, the Headwrap has become popular in recent years because it's easy to wear and care for. Ready-made Headwraps may be simple and casual, or festooned with all sorts of trimmings for evening wear.

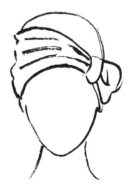

PROFILE HAT

This term refers to any hat on which one side of the brim is turned up to reveal the wearer's profile from the side. The other side may be straight or turned down (as shown).

OFF-FACE HAT

This is a term for any hat whose front brim sweeps up and back from the wearer's forehead.

THE RIGHT HAT
FOR YOUR FEATURES

There's a hat for everyone, designers say. But which one is for you?

"Study your face," Frank Olive advises. "Is it oblong? Square? Do you have a big chin or a tiny one? Is your forehead high or low?" Study your facial size and features carefully, he suggests, before you go into a hat boutique or department store. Will you be looking for an indented crown to lengthen a square face, or something with a wide brim to soften narrow features? Will you need an irregular brim to draw attention from a strong jawline, or a small, off-face brim to lengthen round features or draw attention from a small chin? If you are small and heavy-set, will a shallow Pillbox suit you better than a Toque?

Hats and people are so individual that there are no hard-and-fast rules. But keeping some guidelines in mind will help you figure out which kinds of brims and crowns might offer the best combination for your particular features. The illustrated section of this book offers many specific suggestions later on. For now, here are some general rules of thumb.

SIZE OF FACE AND FEATURES

Facial size and features play an important role in determining the type of hat you can wear best. In general, large hats are for large faces and features; small hats—either close-fitting or with small crowns and proportioned brims—are better for women with small faces or relatively small features. While large-featured women can wear small hats, the faces of small-featured women risk being overpowered by hats with large or wide brims (though this is not always true).

SIZE AND BODY SHAPE

These are the next important factors. Women of medium to tall height (say, 5'5" to 5'10") and average proportions can wear most styles and shapes.

If you are short, or much taller than average (say, 5'11" or taller), or if your proportions are a consideration, here are a few more helpful hints from the experts:

• **Short or petite:** If you are less than 5'5" tall, you may look better in low- or shallow-crowned hats, since high crowns make short people look shorter. Short women should also look for small or proportioned brims (that is, brims whose sizes are relatively narrow in relation to the crown) instead of hats with wide brims (like the Portrait), since wide brims tend to emphasize a lower height.

To look taller (or at least not shorter), try wearing

- Low crowns instead of tall ones
- Indented, sculpted, creased, or draped crowns
- Upswept brims and profile brims

• **Heavyset:** Heavy or full-figured women can wear hats, just as everyone else can; in fact, a pretty hat that emphasizes the eyes and draws attention to the face can have an overall slenderizing effect.

• If you are **tall and full-figured,** look for larger hats with irregular brims that will help balance your figure.

• If you are **short and full-figured,** look for close-fitting hats with small or proportioned brims that will draw attention upward, to your face. Avoid deep, high crowns. (Says designer Marsha Akins: "Stay away from extremes.")

• **Extremely tall and slender:** Height is an advantage in hat wearing, not a drawback, so make the most of what you've got! If you are concerned about appearing too tall, pick hats with shallow crowns and irregular, small-to-medium brims. If you are unusually slender as well as tall, or if you have a small head or a long face (see below), you may prefer to avoid close-fitting, brimless styles like Turbans or brimless Cloches (see photograph on page 52 and illustration on page 7), as well as hats with tall, narrow crowns.

Once again, however, these "rules" are not etched in stone. Proportion has a lot to do with how a hat looks on an individual woman—a well-proportioned woman who is 5'3" may be able to wear a large, drooping brim as well as a taller woman. So use your judgment—and experiment!

FACIAL SHAPE

This is another determining factor. But many hats adapt well to a variety of facial shapes, depending on the angle and position (or "attitude") at which the particular hat is worn. "It's not the shape of the woman's face that really decides," says Frank Olive, "but the attitude of the hat."

Here are some general guidelines to keep in mind. Your face will probably fit (more or less) into one of the categories described. Keep in mind that the hats depicted here and in the illustrated sections later on won't be the *only* styles you can wear.

• **Oval:** Almost any brim will look good on this shape of face. Hats with large brims—straight or floppy—are the most flattering. If you are short or petite, however, look for narrow or proportioned brims rather than large ones.

(Note: Since oval faces can wear so many hats, we mention your shape in the illustrations in Part 2 only if the hat is suited mainly to an oval face.)

• **Round:** A rising crown and an irregular (asymmetrical) brim will add length to your face and prevent it from looking chubby.

• **Square:** A wide, or square, face will appear narrower with an irregular brim and a prominent crown. Setting the hat at an angle will soften square edges.

• **Long:** Widen and soften an oblong face with a full brim. An upswept brim, or a hat with trim that lifts the eye upward, will also soften features. Stay away from tall, narrow shapes.

• **Triangular:** A short asymmetrical brim and high crown will emphasize eyes and draw attention away from a strong jawline, as will a rolled or upswept brim.

Oval

Round

Square

Long

Triangular

Heart-Shaped

- **Heart-shaped:** If your chin is small, draw attention upward with a small hat worn high on the head. Stay away from large, heavy shapes. Trim should lift eye upward.

COLORING, SKIN TEXTURE, AND HAIR STYLE

Usually these are not important factors; however, millinery experts do offer a suggestion or two for certain problems:

- If you have skin blemishes, such as acne scars, they should be covered with a makeup base, since a hat will draw attention to your facial features. You should wear the same makeup to try on hats in the store as you would wear with a hat after you've bought it.

- If your skin is aged, if your complexion is sallow, or if you have shadows under your eyes, don't wear a drooping brim, as the shadow it casts will emphasize these features. Dead-black hats may also emphasize sallow or aged skin.

- Today's natural-looking hair styles allow almost any woman to wear a hat. If you have long, straight hair and like to wear it loose and flowing over the shoulders rather than tied back or tucked behind your ears, a simple Shepherdess or Beret will work best for you; if you like more formal and elaborate clothing styles, wear your hair back, or up, to try on hats.

TRYING IT ON IN THE STORE

And now, equipped with all this information, you are ready for the Big Moment: going to a store and searching for the perfect hat for you. So here's the experts' Rule Number One about trying on hats: *Don't worry about "rules."*

Experiment. Have *fun*.

Try on big hats, small hats, serious hats, silly hats. Try on high and low crowns, irregular brims and symmetrical ones, Caps and Cloches, Portraits and Pillboxes. By trying on all kinds of hats, every which way, you'll become an expert on the only hats that count— the ones that look great on *you*.

BASICS

• If at all possible, wear the clothes you want the hat to complement when you go out to shop for it.

• Be sure the store has a mirror large enough to see your head and shoulders in, as well as a hand mirror for looking at your profile and the back of your head.

PUTTING IT ON

The way you put a hat on is important because its design features are usually created with certain positions, or attitudes, in mind. If you start by putting it on incorrectly, you won't see the hat to full advantage. Here is the correct way to put it on:

1. Look at the hat to see which way it goes. Usually the short end is the back; normally there is also a label inside the back of the sweatband.

2. Holding it as illustrated, look straight ahead at the mirror. Do not tilt your head forward.

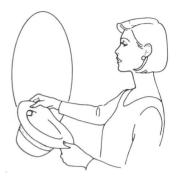

3. Bring the hat up to your forehead, placing the inside front edge on your brow. Now, gently pull the back down with the other hand. This method will keep your hair in place and will position the hat correctly.

Important: Do not plunk the hat down onto the top or back of your crown. Some hats are designed to be worn like a halo, but most, if worn on the back of the head, will give you a naïve, just-in-from-the-hayfield look.

4. Still holding the front brim in place, pull or gently press down on the back brim or crown to secure the hat, as shown. It should fit snugly without pinching anywhere.

THE FIT

A hat that fits is comfortable on your head—it isn't loose, but it also doesn't clamp your brow like a vise. "A hat," says Frank Olive, "should caress your head, not squeeze it. It should touch the forehead without pinching, and the crown of your head should almost touch the inside of the hat's crown, unless the hat is very tall."

"A good indication of fit," advises Patricia Underwood, "is the proportion of the hat's crown to your cheekbones. The sides of the crown should be flush with the outer edges of your cheekbones." (If the crown is wider than your cheekbones, it will dwarf your face; if narrower, you'll look like a pinhead.)

All designers agree that fit is the most important single factor in whether you'll be happy with the hat.

"WORKING" THE HAT

Now look in the mirror to see what adjustments are needed in the hat's attitude. If it seems too far forward, lift the front gently and edge it back a little, as shown.

Most hats should be worn at a slightly sideways angle—say, at least a quarter of an inch—so try tilting it this much or more toward the "down" side, if there is one. (The "down" side is the side that tends to angle downward or to hug your cheek.) Many hats are designed to be tilted toward this side. If you can't tell which is the "down" side, try it both ways; one side will always look better at an angle than the other. "This," Patricia Underwood explains, "will make a hat look much more stylish, because a sideways angle helps to compensate for the irregularities of the human face."

Don't hesitate to "work" the hat. The only way you'll find out how it looks best on you is to try all possible positions. Tilt it even more to see what the effect is at different angles; bring it forward on your brow; try it on sideways and even backwards—sometimes a hat that isn't flattering when worn "correctly" suddenly looks perfect when a particular woman puts it on backward!

Look at the hat from all directions, using a hand mirror to see its effect in profile and from behind. "If you hold it in your hand to look at it," says famed designer Archie Eason, "hold it straight out at eye level—that's the angle from which people will be seeing you in it."

Keep "working" the hat until you've seen it at every possible attitude. You'll know when you've found the right hat and the right position for it—if a hat is for you, it will "announce" the fact as soon as you've found the attitude that makes you cry "That's it!"

LOOK BELOW THE NECK

Finally, if you aren't wearing the clothes you want the hat to complement, visualize what it will look like when you're wearing them. Consider how the neckline and bodice will interact with the hat and how the proportions of the clothing as a whole will be balanced or offset by the proportions of the hat (for example, the way a wide-brimmed Portrait hat might balance or offset a large, loose suit jacket). Does it work with the costume or against it? Does it seem merely tacked on, or does it add an element that the costume doesn't provide?

ASKING THE RIGHT QUESTIONS

Let's assume you and a hat have just fallen madly in love, but you're not yet certain you want a permanent relationship. Here are questions designers suggest you ask yourself when deciding whether to tie the knot:

• Does the design enhance my face? (Don't be fooled by pretty trimmings—remember, look at the overall design and whether it flatters your facial features and your appearance as a whole.)

• How does it look in relation to my height and proportions?

• How much of my wardrobe—including shoes, bags, and other accessories—will it go with? Does it suit my lifestyle? My image of myself?

• How does it interact with what I'm wearing? Does it enhance it, do nothing for it, or work against it?

• If I like the hat but not the way it looks with what I'm wearing, would a different outfit show the hat to better advantage? (For example, would a more open or revealing collar allow it to "breathe" in a way a turtleneck won't? Would a hat that appears plain with small earrings look dramatic with large ones?)

• If the brim emphasizes my eyes, will I need to wear more eye makeup than usual?

TRY ON EVERYTHING YOU LIKE!

Again, the only way you'll develop an eye for hats is by experimenting. So try on all the hats you're interested in. That includes those locked up in the glass case as well as moderately priced, top-of-the-counter hats. And never be afraid to ask all the questions you need to ask. Salespeople expect customers to try on different items before deciding—and in a good store, the staff is paid to advise you as well as to take your money.

TO BUY OR NOT TO BUY?

Eureka—you've found it at last! The hat that suits your face, your wardrobe, your lifestyle, and your pocketbook, and makes you feel like Greta Garbo, Ingrid Bergman, and Meryl Streep rolled into one. It's a terrific hat!

But how do you know if it's a *good* hat?

BEFORE
YOU BUY THAT HAT...

How do you know a good hat from one of lesser quality?

Apart from the designer's or manufacturer's name, which appears inside the crown, you can look at the design and materials. "A fine hat doesn't look as if it just came off the assembly line," says David Stein of Frank Olive's World. "Better hats are designed to give you an individual touch when you wear them." This means that a good hat, worn frequently, will gradually begin to mold itself to the contours of your head in subtle ways. It becomes part of you—though it will also hold its shape better than a cheap hat. An inexpensive, mass-produced hat will lack the suppleness and careful design that permits it to become part of your individual look.

EXAMINE HOW IT'S MADE

A good hat may be moderately priced, but the material—whether wool, felt, suede, straw, fur, or a synthetic—should be relatively soft and supple. High-quality fabrics and dyes also reflect light and color more sensuously than inexpensive materials. The color of a good hat will appear richer, less harsh, than a cheap one.

Examine the hat's features:

- **Materials:**

Fall-winter hats: Usually fur, fur felt, wool felt, or velour. Material should be soft, not brittle or scratchy, and smooth to the touch.

Spring-summer: Usually linen, silk, or straw is used (nylon fibers and synthetic as well as natural straws are also acceptable; straw may be either unpainted or lacquered, but should be flexible, evenly woven, fine-grained, and unbroken).

• **Brim:** Supple (even if it's a rigid brim), not cardboardlike.

• **Sweatband** (the band inside the rim of the hat, usually made of grosgrain ribbon): Should be smoothly sewn, not puckered.

• **Overall shape:** Look at the shape of the hat. Hold it out at arm's length. A well-designed hat will "assert itself," advises milliner David Stein. If it could talk, it would probably say "I'm not this way by accident, you know; somebody *meant* me to look exactly like this."

To train yourself to recognize quality, go to both an inexpensive store that sells hats and to a good department store displaying hats by respected manufacturers and designers of millinery to compare the hats you see in each store. You'll quickly learn to spot the differences.

WHERE TO FIND WELL-MADE HATS

• Better department stores
• Better millinery shops (including chains)
• Thrift shops and antique clothing stores
• Men's shops (for men's styles)
• Hunting and sporting goods stores (especially for men's sporting styles such as safari hats, hunter's hats, etc.)
• Army and Navy stores (military fashions)

WHAT DO I DO
WHEN I GET IT HOME?

Simple. "My first step in buying a hat is to find something I love on *me*," says designer Marsha Akins. "My second step is to *wear* it."

CULTIVATING A RELATIONSHIP

Wear your hat. Take it out of its box and start trying it on with different outfits, jewelry, and accessories. Enjoy it, play with it. You and your hat need to get used to each other. Try wearing it with collars turned up or down, with suits and coats and turtlenecks and silk blouses.

Give it a chance to get to know you, too. Learn to give deft little tugs to your Portraits and Panamas as you adjust the angle, so the brim will become supple and begin to reflect the attitude at which you like to wear it. Grasp the crown of that Fedora firmly when settling it onto your head, kneading the material with your fingers as you do so, so that it can soften and mold itself to your contours. "Any woman can learn to make a hat her own," says David Stein of Frank Olive's World, "a part of her individual fashion look, if she isn't afraid of the hat."

STORING IT

A good hat will last twenty or thirty years if properly cared for. Store your investment neatly and carefully. Hat boutiques usually provide a hatbox at no charge; department stores generally offer collapsible cardboard boxes that can be used for storage. Some department and luggage stores sell permanent collapsible hat boxes of leather, vinyl, or cardboard for storage and transportation.

Store your hat in tissue paper in a box on a shelf. If it's a soft hat, do not roll it up; lay it flat. Put tissue paper inside to help hold the shape. (Styrofoam heads, the kind used to model wigs, are also good for this purpose.)

Never stack good hats one inside another. If you run out of boxes and are desperate for something to store a hat in, suggests designer Marsha Akins, wrap the hat in tissue paper and store it on a shelf in a paper shopping bag without anything else in the bag. Never store hats permanently in plastic food bags, since certain fabrics like fur felt may eventually rot from the humidity generated by heat left from your head. If you must use a large plastic shopping bag as a container, designer Ann Albrizio warns, be sure to poke holes in it, to provide ventilation, and wrap the hat carefully in tissue paper.

Wonderful Hats and How to Wear Them

This section will get you started thinking about the kinds of hats that are your best bets. When studying the drawings in this section, try to visualize how each crown or brim would look on you—with your face's uniquely individual shape and features and with your physical proportions. If a particular size or style isn't your cup of tea, you'll find suggestions for alternative ideas. In no time at all, you'll begin to see possibilities you've never thought of before—and you'll be all set to start your search for your own wonderful hat.

PICTURE THIS FACE....

Nothing draws attention to a woman's face and eyes more swiftly and dramatically than the frame of a beautiful brim designed to do just that. Although the Portrait style naturally comes to mind, it's not the only way to go, as you'll see here.

Beige off-face felt hat with a wide flip brim. *Ideal for:* Square face, prominent chin (upswept brim pulls eye upward; low, snug crown helps balance broad cheekbones), large face and features; with heavy coats, tailored clothing; all daytime occasions—this is a versatile hat. *Notes:* An upswept brim is an advantage to short women, since it lends height. Small-featured women should avoid wide, heavy brims; if the upswept brim is a good choice for you, look for a small, short, or narrow one.

SHOW BIZ

Practically the only thing you can't do in this unusual and versatile leopard-spotted hat is go unnoticed. Moldable into many shapes, here the large brim has been pinned into place with a medal for a buccaneering look. *Ideal for:* Most facial shapes, depending on how the brim is worn. This is a hat for large-featured women. Wear with casual fall and winter coats, big jackets, and lots of swagger. *Notes:* If you are short or your features are small, simply look for a small, flexible hat that will allow you to mold it into dramatic shapes. Flexible hats are widely available and come in many different fabrics, patterns, and designs. (See the "six-way" hat on page 35.)

CHANGING MOODS

This original felt hat with a draped crown and flexible brim is also versatile. It can frame the face several ways, depending on whether the brim is worn up or down. *Ideal for:* Large- and small-featured women. Most facial shapes can wear this hat. (Small features: Wear brim swept up and close to crown.) Most daytime wear; with brim worn up, might be used as a business hat. *Notes:* Draped crowns with brims in upswept position are especially good for short women (both add height).

PROPORTION WITH POISE

A gently tailored, delicate springtime hat with an up-turned, proportioned brim is flattering to small as well as to large features. For petites, a good alternative to the usual Portrait style. *Ideal for:* Oval or long faces. Simple springtime suits, wispy summer dresses, softly tailored blouses. Daytime wear. *Notes:* Short, full-figured women should avoid straight, wide brims like this and opt for small hats with upswept, off-face, and profile brims and shallow crowns.

THE WOMAN WHO'S SEEN IT ALL

What could be more stunning than this gigantic black cart-wheel Portrait? It's bold, dar-ing, sophisticated—a hat to make heads turn. *Ideal for:* Oval or long face; large fea-tures; medium-to-tall height and slender proportions. Sim-ple suits and daytime dresses that won't "fight" the drama of the hat; large, loose jackets that will balance its width. For day-time and outdoor socializing—indoors, this type of hat could be overpowering. *Notes:* Many are called but few are chosen to wear a hat this large. If you are small-featured, short, unusually tall, or other than slender, you'll be better off finding a picture hat with a smaller or proportioned brim.

PRETTY BUSINESS

Hats are image makers. Whatever your line of work, a hat will sharpen your looks, confidence, and leverage at business luncheons or meetings. Any of the hats in this section can give you a winning edge.

Drop-dead, super-glamorous white felt Cloche with indented crown, a feather, and a touch of Marlene Dietrich. *Ideal for:* Long faces (because of full brim), round and square faces (because of prominent crown); large features. Slightly masculine touch makes this perfect with tweeds and other tailored wool suits. A versatile hat for all daytime business. *Notes:* Observe that model wears this hat well forward on brow for a private look but angled a few degrees toward "down" side, to soften and offset hat's slight severity.

VERY MUCH A LADY

This simple white straw profile Cloche is another classic style that many women feel comfortable with. *Ideal for:* Oval and some square and triangular faces (because of irregular brim and rising crown—however, check "down" side in profile to be sure it doesn't overemphasize jawline). Short or petite women. Most business suits and daytime dresses. *Notes:* Wear angled toward "down" side.

SPORTING FELLOW

This black felt Derby is a slightly "masculine" business hat that will offset and balance tweeds, woolens, or elegant sportswear. *Ideal for:* Triangular and heart-shaped faces (upturned brim and high crown draw attention from jawline or small chin); small features (short brim); if crown is relatively shallow, good for short or petite women. Tailored suits and jackets, soft wool sweaters, etc. *Notes:* Wear at a slight side angle and forward on brow.

A HINT OF FLASH

This silver-gray straw Gaucho is a simple daytime hat whose metallic finish and Spanish-style crown lend a touch of flair to a costume otherwise all business. *Ideal for:* Long or square faces. Almost any daytime clothing. *Notes:* Hat is angled slightly to side (about a quarter-inch) to soften lines of face and offset symmetry of glasses.

If you wear glasses, be sure that your hats leave eyebrows showing a little so that your eyes are not obscured.

FRIENDLY AND FEMININE

Another highly flexible daytime hat, this burnt-orange felt is versatile enough to suit almost any face, wardrobe, or daytime occasion. Because the brim is designed to be molded several different ways, this hat can be worn in a variety of shapes and attitudes. For this reason, it is known as a "six-way hat." *Ideal for:* Virtually all faces, depending on how you mold the brim and the attitude you give the hat. Will soften man-tailored suits and coats. *Notes:* A good hat for short women (deep, close crown does not reduce height) and women with small features (flexible brim provides a proportioned "frame" effect).

Notice that wearing brim up to reveal eyebrows creates an open, friendly look.

ASSERTIVE BUT WOMANLY

A sexy felt Fedora like this one, with its heavily indented crown, is just masculine enough to make everyone notice that you're a lady. *Ideal for:* Many business outfits, from softly draped jersey dresses with cashmere scarves to man-tailored tweeds. Worn at a slight tilt (as shown) and with the crown indentation somewhat off-center, a carefully chosen Fedora can be wonderful for a round, square, or triangular face. *Notes:* If face is round or triangular, choose small Fedoras. A wide brim (but not a tall, narrow crown) may be good for some long faces. Small-featured women and women with heart-shaped faces should exercise discretion with Fedoras—a high, heavy crown or a wide brim may overpower these faces.

THE BEAUTIFUL BERET

French and flirty, the Beret is a perennial favorite. Basically it's just a bag turned upside down and drawn tight at the mouth. But if its origins are humble, its varieties are astonishing.

GLITTERGIRL

Pretty and striking, jeweled Berets—like this soft white leather one with brass studs and rhinestones—are common and come in many different sizes, materials, and colors. *Ideal for:* Round, heart-shaped, and triangular faces. Will add som flash to casual wear or a dress for a date. *Notes:* for almost any facial shap *Notes* for "Simply Classic." in different attitudes.

Do *not* wear jeweled hats—including leather ones—with jeans, leather bomber jackets, etc.

SIMPLY CLASSIC

The basic wool beret is never out of fashion. *Ideal for:* round and heart-shaped faces (but any facial shape can usually wear this style); any height or proportion. Casual wear, indoors and out. *Notes:* Unusually tall, slender women and women with square or long faces should look for wider Berets and wear them at an irregular attitude; triangular faces should also wear irregularly to offset a strong jawline.

If you wear a Beret straight (as shown), it tends to look demure; if at a strong angle, flirty or rakish.

SASS AND DASH

W ant to put more punch into your casual
outfits? These jaunty men's styles
will jazz up ordinary coats, sweaters, and jackets
and make admiring eyes swivel your way.

A felt cap that says, "Salute me, I'm pretty!" *Ideal for:* Round, square, and long faces; small features. A versatile casual daytime hat. *Notes:* Wear well forward and at an angle, not straight or back on the crown.

If your hair is thick and curly, here's proof that you don't have to crop those tresses to look terrific in a good hat.

COWPOKE

The classic Western—here's one in felt with a feathered band—is a hat that can pull together many casual costumes. *Ideal for:* Round, square, and long faces; large features; medium height. *Notes:* Westerns come in many varieties. If your face is long, look for a wide brim like this one, but with a relatively wide, shallow crown. If it is heart-shaped, or if you are short or petite, try to find smaller crowns and proportioned brims (avoid large, heavy Western styles like ten-gallon hats). If you have small features, look for shallow crowns and as short a brim as possible in a Western.

RACY DAME

Off to the track in a visored gray felt Groom's Cap that's perfect for any informal coat or jacket. *Ideal for:* Long faces; small features; petites. Good for any casual outdoor occasion. *Notes:* Wear well forward on brow and angle crown to the side. Round and triangular faces: A low-visored cap may make your face look chubby or your jaw extra-prominent. Look instead for a Cap or Beret with a rising crown and a short visor.

READY FOR ACTION

Just for fun: A vintage black-leather "ace" flyer's helmet lined with sheepskin for high-altitude aviation. *Ideal for:* A small, slender face and delicate features (because it's close to the head). Cold-weather casual gear—wear (of course) with a leather flight jacket. *Notes:* Vintage or novelty hats of many different kinds can turn up in all sorts of places. Look not only in military surplus stores but also in thrift shops, antique clothing stores, and Americana-collector shops.

A BIT OF BRASS

Even if you're the girl next door, this high-toned black military Cap with white braid will add spit-and-polish to your outfit. *Ideal for:* Long, triangular, and heart-shaped faces (high front pulls eye up and away from a strong jaw or small chin). Wear this with something audacious—army camouflage, a jacket with shiny epaulettes, a swirling wool cape. *Notes:* Round and square faces: Look for a hat with a shorter visor to avoid shortening and widening face. Wear forward on the brow, not back.

Military hats are usually available at Army and Navy surplus stores or military-collector shops.

FEMME FATALE

F eeling sultry? Here are two different styles famed for their power to beguile and to make their wearer feel like the siren temptress she is at heart.

COQUETTE

A soft, slouchy Beret like this one should be worn to the side if you want a youthful, flirtatious look. *Ideal for:* Virtually all faces, depending on how it is worn; large and small features; all heights. Goes with most daytime and casual evening wear (for evening, wear pendant earrings). *Notes:* If your face is oval or long, you can wear it pulled down over the ear on one side, as shown; if round, square, triangular, or heart-shaped, see how this style looks worn higher on the head with a sideways tilt, and the brim pulled slightly forward over the brow.

SIREN SONG

Turbans, like this one in white nylon, always confer a hint of the mysterious East. *Ideal for:* Oval, long, and heart-shaped faces (if wrap draws eye upward, as with the Turban shown here). A well-made Turban in a good knit, silk, or nylon will add fascination to many daytime or evening outfits, from a slinky jersey dress to a satin dinner suit like this one. *Notes:* If your features are small or your face is round, square, or triangular, stay away from full Turban styles and look instead for a Headwrap with an asymmetrical effect (see "Summer Coolers," page 63), perhaps with a small bow or jewel on top to draw the eye upward.

AN AFTERNOON AFFAIR

S hopping, drinks, a matinee—or something more amorous? Here are hats to make you feel rich, sophisticated, and alluring. What you do in them is up to you.

Black-and-white straw Portrait with two romantic flowers that mirror each other like water lilies on a pond. *Ideal for:* Oval and long faces; large features. Wear with soft silk and linen suits and dresses or a light spring coat. *Notes:* Sparkling earrings will add to the glamor. Small-featured, short, and petite women should look for a strong, simple design with a proportioned brim.

PLAYFUL OR PRIVATE

A versatile "flapper" Cloche of creamy felt. If brim is worn off the face (as shown), mood is open and playful; worn down, mood is mysterious and seductive. *Ideal for:* heart-shaped face (wear brim up); small features; any height (especially good for short or petite women). Daytime suits, dresses, and coats; some evening wear (add large, glittery earrings). *Notes:* If you have a round face or a weak or heavy jawline, a flapper style may emphasize this. Be sure to check profile when trying on this style.

A BURST OF INDISCRETION?

The pleated sunburst on this otherwise demure yellow straw Profile hat for spring just hints at the possibility. *Ideal for:* Square and long faces; large features; medium height. Tailored light coats, suits, dresses. *Notes:* Round, triangular, and heart-shaped faces and short and petite women should look for a profile hat with a shorter brim and trim that draws eye upward.

CROWNING GLORY

This remarkable red felt Scottie, with its extravagant bow, delicate veil, and spray of feathers, is the last word in splendid sophistication for afternoons out. *Ideal for:* heart-shaped faces (draws eye from a small chin); small features. Keep costume simple and slender with a heavily trimmed hat like this. *Notes:* Wear well forward on brow and at a slight sideways angle, as shown. Short, heavy-set, and very tall women may want to look for a small, pretty Scottie or Pillbox with more restrained trimming—fewer feathers or a smaller veil.

ETERNALLY ELEGANT

Sensuous to the touch and trimmed with a spray of ostrich feathers, this always-fashionable, "Princess Di" Pillbox in wine-red velvet can be worn for both late afternoon and evening occasions, depending on the clothes. *Ideal for:* Round, triangular, and heart-shaped faces (wear forward and at a slight sideways angle); small features; slender, short, and petite women. *Notes:* Extremely short or tall or full-figured women might look for an untrimmed version of this hat that will not emphasize height—for example, a plain red-velvet Pillbox or a velvet Beret style.

TOAST OF THE TOWN

Whether it's for dinner or dancing—or just for letting someone know that going out with him is a special event—these hats will add glamour and excitement to gala evenings.

Extravagant rhinestone-spangled teardrop ("Alexis") Cap with a jeweled veil. The teardrop Cap is flattering to virtually any woman, whatever her size, height, or facial features. *Ideal for:* Glittery occasions after eight—keep dress and jewelry simple, since a hat like this *is* your jewelry. *Notes:* If your face is square or long, wear hat off center, as shown. Triangular: Wear higher and off center to draw eye upward, away from jawline. Round or heart-shaped: Wear high, with point of cap centered, to add length to face.

WOMAN OF THE WORLD

An unusual and sophisticated swirl, this Fez made of black feathers should be worn with large, important jewelry and your simplest and most expensive little dinner suit or evening jacket. *Ideal for:* All but long faces; small-featured women; medium height. Perfect for a nightclub or a special dinner. *Notes:* Wear forward on the brow and slightly to the side, as shown. Short and petite women: You can also achieve this understated, but glamorous, effect with a shallower black evening hat, perhaps a sequined Beret or Pillbox style.

SWEET AND SMART

Here is a versatile cocktail or evening hat—a straw Pillbox in soft gray with a big pearl-gray scalloped ruffle on the side. *Ideal for:* All except long faces; small features. Medium height is best, but may also be worn by short women (see below). Demure and smart, this hat could be worn not only with a fancy dinner dress and sparkling jewelry, but also with a dressy suit or a soft, clinging jersey knit for late-afternoon cocktails.

Notes: The asymmetry of this hat's design (the large ruffle on one side) makes it good for many round, square, and heart-shaped faces. On the other hand, if you are quite short or if your features are tiny, make sure a large decoration, such as this ruffle, doesn't look out of proportion to your height or face. If it does, look for a shallower Pillbox style and less heavy trim.

FESTIVE FEZ

Charming, fun, and strictly for the gala evenings in your life, this unusual cone-shaped hat with a gold pom-pom cries out for full regalia—gown, careful makeup, important jewelry. *Ideal for:* Round, square, triangular, and heart-shaped faces (receding crown and pom-pom pull the eye upward to add length to face; wear forward and angled about a quarter-inch to one side); small features; medium height. *Notes:* Very tall, short, and heavy-set women: This shape is too tall and narrow for you. As an alternative, try a small black-velvet cap with jeweled trim, or a hair decoration made of a black cap and gold netting, worn at the back of the head or at the nape of the neck.

WINTER WARMERS

W hy settle for shapeless knit caps or earmuffs to keep your head warm? Stylish hats like the ones in this section combine comfort, warmth, and class for the cold months of fall and winter.

A magnificent rhinestone-studded black-velour helmet Cloche, with matching black gloves. *Ideal for:* Oval, square, and long faces; good for small features as well as large faces; any height. Rising effect of crown also makes this a good hat for some wide faces, or for women with a strong jawline. For swanky dinners and other glittering occasions. *Notes:* Round, triangular, and heart-shaped faces might prefer a rolled or upswept Cloche with an asymmetrical brim, or a shallower hat worn high on the head.

AUTUMN PLUMAGE

The peaked crest of this delightful Pillbox was inspired by the helmets of Tartar warriors, but the feathers make it a whimsically feminine creation for autumn wear. *Ideal for:* Triangular and heart-shaped faces; small features; petites. Luscious with a feathered boa like the one shown here, but would be just as pretty with a simple wool coat or a tailored suit. An elegant and dressy daytime hat. *Notes:* Wear well forward on the brow and angled toward the "down" side, as shown.

GENTLE AS A LAMB

Soft and pliant, this gray Persian-lamb Beret is timelessly fashionable as well as luxurious. *Ideal for:* Round, square, and triangular faces (rising crown adds length); small and large features; any height. An all-occasion outdoor hat. *Notes:* Hats made of materials like Persian lambswool provide a beautiful and striking alternative to the choice between inexpensive wools and expensive furs—and a hat like this will last forever.

SHAMELESSLY PAMPERED

With its matching muff and fur boa, this glorious dark-brown fox Beret, tied with a black ribbon band, is every woman's dream of a snuggly fur hat. *Ideal for:* Almost all facial shapes and features. A street hat for both daytime and evening warmth. *Notes:* If you are short or plump, look instead for a flattering short-haired fur hat that does not completely envelop the head and that leaves a little hair showing.

SPRING FEVER

A glorious spring hat—the very essence of romance and femininity. Here are five that will inspire you to find one that best becomes the reawakened woman.

The queen of Easter bonnets, a Shepherdess brim of linen straw overlaid with lace and crowned with an Imperial rose and taffeta bow. *Ideal for:* Oval, square, and long faces; large features; medium height. Perfect for diaphanous lawns, puffed shoulders, and strapless warm-weather frocks. A hat for May garden parties and June weddings. *Notes:* Women with round, triangular, and heart-shaped faces or small features, and petite, short, or heavy-set women: A tiny, lacy cap—or a small hat with a short or upswept brim, lightly trimmed in similar materials—will set an equally romantic note without overpowering facial features or exaggerating short or heavy proportions.

PRETTY LASS

This dainty straw Boater with
its molded crown and orna-
mental flower evokes thoughts
of picnics on grassy river banks.
Ideal for: Triangular and heart-
shaped faces; small features;
short and petite women. Pretty
batiste blouses and cotton
frocks. Perfect for—what
else?—boating on the lake or
strolling in the park. *Notes:* If
you are short or petite, look for
Boaters with small brims; if
you have a long face, look for
wider brims. Setting this hat at
a strong sideways angle will
offset chubbiness in round faces
and soften the edges of square
ones.

Wear a Boater or Sailor forward on the brow (as shown),
not back on the crown.

MY FAIR LADY

This white Portrait with its see-
through brim is sparely
trimmed but serenely sentimen-
tal. *Ideal for:* Oval and long
faces; large features; medium-
to-tall height. Best with soft,
draped, or unfussy flowing materials that will echo the fragil-
ity of the hat and balance its
size. A classic spring and summer outdoor hat for garden
parties and weddings. *Notes:* If
your facial shape or features, or
your physical size or proportions, make a small, narrow-
brimmed hat a better choice,
try a small, white Cloche with a
simple white veil and a delicate
brim for a similar effect.

NINE-TO-FIVE SPRING FLING

This splendid peacock-blue straw Profile hat with its scalloped split brim and peacock feather turns a restrained, even severe business costume into a celebration of the season. *Ideal for:* Oval, square, and long faces; large features; medium height. Tailored daytime clothes. *Notes:* Women with small features can wear an elaborate spring hat just as well as women with large ones if the brim is proportioned. A short-brimmed profile hat similar to this would be flattering to round, triangular, and heart-shaped faces (because of the upswept, irregular brim).

BLOSSOM TIME

An elegant and graceful Portrait for daytime suits and dresses. *Ideal for:* Oval and long faces; large features; medium height. Use a heavily trimmed hat like this to balance and add interest to simple cottons, silks, and linens (if the outfit is too frilly, it will compete with the hat). *Notes:* Look at this hat carefully and you'll see that, as with any good hat, it's not just the flowers that make it pretty, but the strong, simple design beneath the trim.

If the Portrait style pictured here isn't ideal for your facial features and size, look instead for a smaller flowered hat—perhaps one with an irregular brim—that flatters your face better. But keep in mind that a good design, rather than trim alone, is what does the job!

SUMMER COOLERS

Casual hats of lightweight or flexible straw, linen, cotton, or canvas will shade your brow, protect you from the sun, and keep you feeling fashionably cool when warm weather comes. Many are versatile as well.

Straw roll-brimmed hat with a Derby crown, exquisitely trimmed with lace. *Ideal for:* Oval, square, and long faces. Lightweight summer suits, sundresses, strapless gowns. A delightful hat for casual evening wear as well as daytime. *Notes:* Short and petite women, look for a short, rolled brim and a low crown.

STRAW ROADSTER

A popular and long-lasting style with women of all face-shapes, sizes, and ages. With the tie knotted at the throat, perfect for a spin along a country road or sailing on a windy day. Tied back behind the nape of the neck, a pretty beach hat or one to wear on a shopping expedition to town. *Notes:* Wear forward on brow and at a slight angle. Short and petite women: Look for this style in a proportioned brim.

TROPICAL HAT WITH OPEN CROWN

A practical and comfortable choice for the woman who wants to keep a cool head. With the addition of jewelry, this is a pretty style for casual summer evening wear, too. *Notes:* Wide, modified Coolie brim shown here is best for oval and long faces and for large features. Women with small features and short or petite women should look for a similar hat with either a proportioned or a fairly straight, short brim.

PAINTED BASEBALL CAP

This fanciful version of a casual American perennial is a pretty attention-getter at the beach or ballpark. *Notes:* An oval or long face is best for a long-visored Cap. Small-featured women should look for short-visored Caps. With the right visor, this is a good style for short or petite women.

HEADWRAP

Feminine and versatile, Headwraps are adaptable enough to flatter any facial shape or size. They can be worn by women of all proportions. Simply add important earrings to transform from beachwear to partywear for a casual summer event. *Notes:* Round, square, long, and triangular faces—wear asymmetrically, as shown. Heart-shaped faces—wear high on the head.

HATIQUETTE: A HATECHISM

Hat etiquette is a matter of good manners and good sense. Here are answers to some of the most frequently asked questions at the millinery counters.

Q. What types of hats are for fall and winter, and what types are for spring and summer?

A. Materials and trimmings will tell you. Fur, felts, velour, velvet, and other warm materials are for fall and winter; straw, silk, stretched linen, and other light materials are for spring and summer (including dark colors). Hats made entirely of feathers are for fall; hats with flowers on them are for spring and summer.

Q. When is a hat for daytime wear and when is it for evening?

A. The inimitable Judith Martin—Miss Manners—has given the world this unsurpassable answer in her *Guide to Excruciatingly Correct Behavior:* "The general rule is that if the hat looks as if you had it built, it may properly go to daytime functions; if it looks as if it just landed in your hair (tiny bits of feathers, sequins, or whatever), it goes out at night." There may be, of course, some late-afternoon to early-evening overlap (see pages 47, 50).

Q. Is it all right for a woman to wear a hat indoors?

A. Perfectly all right. (Men are the ones who have to take their hats off indoors.) The exceptions: In your own home or your own office. Wearing a hat implies that you are on your way to or from somewhere and, therefore, that you are not giving those around you (guests, colleagues) your full attention.

Q. Can I wear a hat to a business meeting?

A. Yes, if you are visiting someone else's office outside your own building—but not in your own office.

Q. I travel a lot on business. Can I wear a hat on an airplane?

A. Certainly. In fact, thirty years ago, when an airplane ride was still a big deal, no "lady" would have dreamed of getting on a plane without a hat. Here is some advice from one seasoned traveler: Wear a hatpin and stow a plastic bag with holes punched in it in your handbag. If you want to nap, put the hat in the plastic bag and pin the bag to the seat in front of you—that way the hat won't interfere with your nap and also won't be crushed.

Q. Should I take my hat off in a restaurant, or check it in the coatroom?

A. Not necessary, unless it's a rainhat or a very warm hat that would be uncomfortable to wear indoors. But if you wore it because you want to look pretty and interesting, why take it off just when the fun's about to start?

Q. What should I do with a veil that covers my face when I'm eating?

A. Lay the veil gracefully back over the brim or crown and let it languish there until you depart. Otherwise, you will be dining on Veil Stew.

Q. What about wearing a hat to the theater, a movie, or a concert?

A. A small afternoon or evening hat—i.e., one that is close to the head and has no trimming that will interfere with the view of those seated behind you—is acceptable. But if it's going to add at all to your height or the width of your head, you should remove the hat during the performance. (Consider how *you'd* feel if you paid what a ticket costs these days and somebody's hat blocked your view!)

Q. Is it all right to wear a hat with trousers?

A. There is no hard-and-fast rule about this. Obviously, you wouldn't wear an elaborate, formal hat with trousers, but you might get away with a small, casual Beret, a Cap, or another simple, informal style. The rule of thumb is: If it looks natural with the outfit, why not?

Q. I love those old-fashioned hats with fruit-and-flower trimmings. But are they in good taste?

A. The answer depends on where you live and what other people wear there. If it's the done thing in your community, then wear and enjoy. (On the other hand, if you're a young, urban working woman, you'll probably find that your peers go in for strong, simple designs, spare on the trimmings.)

Q. Is it correct to wear a black (or a white) hat to a wedding?

A. A black hat is fine if the hat looks festive, not funereal, and is worn with a bright outfit. Keep the total ensemble in mind—it should be celebratory, not somber.

On the other hand, don't wear a white hat that makes you look like the bride, if you aren't.

Q. I am about to marry for the second time. Should I wear a hat or a veil?

A. A hat, not a veil, is the correct and appropriate headwear for the bride the second time around.

Q. I love hats, but they flatten my hair and make my head itch. Is there a polite way to handle this problem?

A. Yes—bolt for the nearest powder room and scratch like mad. Then start buying hats that fit. The itching is probably due to the added heat and perspiration generated by a hat that's too small.

Q. Is it appropriate to wear a hat if you wear glasses?

A. Of course. Just wear glasses—and hats—that show as much of your eyes as possible. (See page 34.)

Q. May one use a hat to hide one's hair when it is in need of attention?

A. One may. One often does.

Q. Is a hat an appropriate gift for a relative or friend?

A. A hat is a great gift, but a highly individual matter. If you think that a hat is something the recipient would enjoy, buy a gift certificate at a good department store and make that your present, explaining that you thought she might have fun picking out an attractive hat for herself. If she says she would, give her a copy of this book as well. Then you'll be sure she knows what she's doing.

HATTACHMENTS

HATPINS

Hatpins can be charming decorations as well as a means of keeping your headgear from flying off in the wind. Position hatpins where the hair is thickest under the hat, or on one side of the crown. You can leave them in place when you store the hat, or stick them in a pretty pincushion as an ornament on your vanity table. Many, like the one on the front of the pincushion shown here, come with a pinguard as well.

Decorative hatpins like those shown here are available at department store millinery counters and in specialty shops.

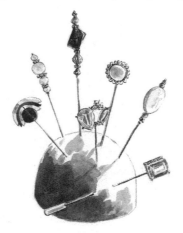

ELASTIC BANDS

If there is an elastic band inside the hat to help hold it in place, the band goes in back, under the hair at the nape of the neck—*not* under your chin.

COMBS

Fine hats sometimes come with little combs sewn to the inside hatband to be used as fasteners instead of—or in addition to—hatpins or an elastic band. Tuck these combs into the hair around your temples or the sides of your head.

TRIMMINGS

Generally, the only addition a good hat needs is your head. Apart from hatpins, which may be decorative, designers advise against adding trimmings to any but the plainest hats. And even though the hat may be simple, if it's well designed, its intended effect may be ruined by the addition of unnecessary ornaments.

If feathers, flowers, ribbons, veils, or sequins are your thing, look for hats on which these trimmings are already a part of the design, rather than trying to add them yourself.

HAT CHECK:
CARE AND CLEANING

Fortunately, hats require only minimal regular care to give years of life.

ORDINARY CARE

Millinery experts advise dusting hats regularly with a clean, soft brush or a clean, static-free cloth. Hats pick up dust and grime out-doors, especially in the city, so brush often.

CLEANING

If properly stored and cared for, your hat should rarely, if ever, need cleaning during its lifetime. Never wash good hats, as they will shrink, and never have them dry cleaned, as this will destroy the wire in the brim. If you feel that your hat needs professional cleaning, take it either to a milliner who also cleans and renovates hats, or to a dry cleaner who is able to send it to such a specialist.

You can clean and give freshening treatments to your own hats, too. The method depends on the material.

• **Felt, velour, or velvet:** A clean, damp sponge, well wrung out, will remove surface dirt from these fabrics.

A good beauty treatment to fluff up the nap of a felt hat is to steam the fabric with a kettle or steam-iron spout. Start with the crown, says designer Ann Albrizio, and work down to the brim, brushing with a clean brush each time you put down the source of steam. Be careful not to get the hat so wet that it will shrink.

For more heavily soiled wool or fur felt, velour, or velvet, brush vigorously with a stiff, clean brush (a new hairbrush, for example) and then try the damp-sponge treatment.

Marsha Akins advises that fur felt—but not wool felt—may be brushed very gently with fine jeweler's sandpaper for heavy grime.

Stains may be treated with cleaning fluid or spray according to manufacturer's directions.

• **Straw:** Natural, synthetic, and lacquered straw hats should be kept well brushed; this will also keep them more rain-resistant. Straw hats may be cleaned with a soapy cloth or sponge soaked in mild detergent, well wrung out. Rinse with a clean damp sponge or cloth, also well wrung out. Straw, like other fabrics, will shrink even if it is lacquered—do not soak the material.

Alma Chesnut Moore's *How to Clean Everything* (Simon and Schuster, 1977) recommends brightening the color and gloss of faded dark straw by rubbing the hat with a dark cloth. Moisten the cloth with one part alcohol to four parts of water, then polish the hat lightly with a piece of dark velvet. "Limp straws can be stiffened by brushing them over with a light coat of clear shellac, diluted with an equal amount of alcohol."

• **Stretched linen:** Follow directions for straw hats.

• **Silk:** If the silk is washable, use a damp sponge as directed under "Felt, velour, or velvet." If you don't know whether it is washable or not, take the hat to a professional.

• **Hat bands** (outer bands and sweatbands): These are usually grosgrain, taffeta, satin, or silk. They can be cleaned with a cleaning fluid or spray according to manufacturer's directions.

If you are in any doubt about the fabric, call the store where you bought it or take it to a good dry cleaner or milliner (men's or women's) before attempting to clean it yourself in order to find out what the fabric is and what kind of treatment is safe.